Silverlight

Interview Questions

You'll Most Likely Be Asked

Second Edition

Job Interview Questions Series

VP **Vibrant Publishers**

www.vibrantpublishers.com

Silverlight Interview Questions
You'll Most Likely Be Asked

Second Edition

ISBN-10: 1461092434
ISBN-13: 978-14-61092-43-8

Library of Congress Control Number: 2011927397

This publication is designed to provide accurate and authoritative information in regard to the subject matter covered. The author has made every effort in the preparation of this book to ensure the accuracy of the information. However, information in this book is sold without warranty either expressed or implied. The Author or the Publisher will not be liable for any damages caused or alleged to be caused either directly or indirectly by this book.

Vibrant Publishers books are available at special quantity discount for sales promotions, or for use in corporate training programs. For more information please write to **bulkorders@vibrantpublishers.com**

Please email feedback / corrections (technical, grammatical or spelling) to **spellerrors@vibrantpublishers.com**

To access the complete catalogue of Vibrant Publishers, visit **www.vibrantpublishers.com**

Table of Contents

This page is intentionally left blank

Silverlight Interview Questions

Review these typical interview questions and think about how you would answer them. Read the answers listed; you will find best possible answers along with strategies and suggestions.

This page is intentionally left blank

Overview of Silverlight

1: How will you load "XAML" into the memory used by your application?

Answer:

Using InitialComponent Method, which is present in the App class method. The partial class templates are implemented by this InitialComponent method which loads the XAML file into the application's memory using 'Load Component' method.

2: What are the events registered in the constructor of App.xaml.cs?

Answer:

The events registered are:
   a) Application_Startup
   b) Application_Exit
   c) Application_UnhandledException

3: Where is InitialComponent () Method implemented?

Answer:

The call to InitialComponent method is made from the Constructor of the App class. However the definition of that class will not be there and is implemented inside the "partial class of App class". i.e) partial implementation of the App class is done in the file called 'App. g. I. Cs'.

4: How will you get the "App.g.i.cs" file in "my_solution?

Answer:

Since this file is an auto generated file by the compiler, it will be automatically placed in a temporary directory labelled "obj". This file will also be available in the "my solution". If it is not found in the My Solution, the solution has to be rebuilt. After that, the App.g.i.cs file will be created.

5: List out the properties that needs to be initialized when a Silverlight control is created using createSilverlight function.

Answer:

   a) Source $\longrightarrow$ xaml or .aspx file

b) elementId $\longrightarrow$ String that identifies the file

6: Which xml files are created when a new project is created in Silverlight?

Answer:

The xml files that are created when a new project is created in Silverlight are:

a) **App.xaml:** contains the declaration of shared resources and handles the global application level event

b) **mainPage.xaml:** default page in silverlight application

7: What is the purpose of 'RootVisual Property'?

Answer:

a) The default page of the Silverlight application is 'mainPage.xaml'

b) To change the default page, 'Rootvisual' property is set in the App.xaml file(Application startup event)

8: What events are handled by Silverlight?

Answer:

The events handled by Silverlight are:

a) **Input event:** Browser handles the input event and send that to the Silverlight plug-in

b) **Non-input event:** Handles events like state change or lifetime information of an object

9: How will you display the Silverlight application in Fullscreen mode?

Answer:

We can display the Silverlight application in Fullscreen mode by setting the 'IsFullscreen' property to 'True'

Example:

Application.Current.Host.Content.my_proprty1 = my_value11'

my_proprty1 $\longrightarrow$ IsFullScreen

my_value11 $\longrightarrow$ True/False

10: Describe about .xap file.

Answer:

a) It is a compiled silverlight application
b) Contains the required files like manifest file, dll file etc to run the application

11: What will happen when F5 is pressed to run the silverlight project?

Answer:

When the application is executed for the first time, a new folder named 'ClienBin' will be created and contains the compiled project.

Laying out a User Interface

12: What is the default value for a Grid's row height and column width?
   a) Auto
   b) 1 px
   c) *
   d) 0 px
Answer:
C

13: If you have a Button inside a Grid that has multiple rows, how do you set the row that the current button will be placed on?
Answer:
Grid.Row="X"

14: How do you set one row of the Grid to be twice the size of another?
Answer:
By setting the Height="1*" and "2*" on the RowDefinitions
<RowDefinition Height="1*"></RowDefinition>
<RowDefinition Height="2*"></RowDefinition>

15: If you have a Button inside a Grid, and did not specify any Grid.Row property on the button, what will the default value be?
Answer:
The default value will be 0.

16: How can you tell a control to span over multiple rows of a Grid?
Answer:
We can tell a control to span over multiple rows of a Grid by setting the Grid.RowSpan="X"

17: What layout control would best fit the following behavior: Its children are ordered one after another without the need to do

any other alignment?
Answer:
Stackpanel layout control.

18: What is the default orientation of a Stackpanel, Vertical or Horizontal?
Answer:
The default orientation of Stackpanel is Vertical.

19: How do you set a button to be placed exactly 10 pixels from the top of its Canvas parent?
Answer:
Canvas.Top=10

20: Inside a canvas, how do you set one control to be on top of another?
Answer:
By specifying the Canvas.ZIndex property (bigger for the control who should be on top)

21: How many children can a Border control have?
Answer:
1 Child.

22: What is the property that you use if you want to set the thickness of a Border control?
Answer:
BorderThickness

23: How do you draw the border line outside the border's bounding box?
Answer:
By specifying a negative value for BorderThickness

24: How do you set the distance between a border and its child?
Answer:

By specifying the Padding property, we can set the distance between a border and its child.

25: What control resizes its content by its own size?
Answer:
Viewbox control resizes its content by its own size.

26: What are the possible values for the VerticalAlignment property?
Answer:
Top, Bottom, Stretch, Center are the possible values.

27: What are the possible values for the HorizontalAlignment property?
Answer:
Left, Right, Stretch, Center are the possible values.

28: How do you set a Textbox's text to be Readonly in XAML?
Answer:
By setting IIsReadOnly="True"

29: What is the property that you have to set to make a Checkbox a three state checkbox?
Answer:
IsThreeState="True"

30: Name some Content controls.
Answer:
Label, Button, CheckBox, RadioButton are some Content Controls.

31: What is the method you use to switch pages if you are using the Navigation Framework?
Answer:
Navigate (Uri uri)

32: How do you set the Title of the browser window if you are

using the Navigation Framework?
Answer:
By specifying the Title Property of the current Page control

33: How do you access the query string of the current page if you are using the Navigation Framework?
Answer:
By using NavigationContext.QueryString[key]

34: What is the property of a ListBox that specifies what Field of the listbox's ItemSource is shown to the user?
Answer:
DisplayMemberPath

35: How can you modify the look of every item in a ListBox?
Answer:
By using the ItemTemplate property, we can modify the look of every item in a ListBox.

36: How do you specify a Listbox to have a Vertical and Horizontal Scrollbar?
Answer:
The Listbox has automatic scrollbars by default.

37: How do you set the distance between the current control and its parent?
Answer:
By using the Margin Property, we can set the distance between current control and its parent.

38: In a DataGrid, how do you specify that each other row has a different highlight color?
Answer:
By using the AlternatingRowBackground="Color" property

39: How do you set the visibility of a DataGrid's horizontal

Scroll Bar?
Answer:
By specifying the HorizontalScrollBarVisibility property

40: In a DataGrid, how can you allow the user to automatically sort columns?
Answer:
By using the CanUserSortColumns="True" property

41: What control can you use to play a video?
Answer:
MediaElement, with its Source="movie.wmv"

42: How do you set the text color of a TextBox to Blue?
Answer:
<TextBox Foreground="Blue" Text="blue text"/>

43: How do you set the text inside a TextBox to be Bold?
Answer:
<TextBox FontWeight="Bold" Text="bold text"/>

44: How do you set the Width of a TextBox to 150?
Answer:
<TextBox Width="150" Text="text"/>

45: How do you set the Height of a TextBox to be based on the size of its contents?
Answer:
<TextBox Height="Auto" Text="text"/>

46: How do you place a TextBlock inside a Grid on the third Row?
Answer:
<TextBlock Grid.Row="2" />

47: How do you place a TextBlock inside a Grid on the first

Column?
Answer:
<TextBlock Grid.Column="0" />

48: You have a Grid with 2 rows and 5 columns. How can you make a TextBlock span on the columns 3 and 4 of the Grid?
Answer:
<TextBlock Grid.Column="2" Grid.ColumnSpan="2" />

49: What does the Margin Property represent?
Answer:
It represents the distance from the current control to its surrounding ones on the four directions (up, down, right, left)

50: When using the Margin property like this Margin="1,2,3,4", in what order will the margins be applied to the four directions (up, down, right, left) ?
Answer:
Left=1,
Top=2,
Right=3,
Down=4

51: When using the Margin property like this Margin="5", what will the values of the four directions (up, down, right, left) be?
Answer:
Left=5,
Top=5,
Right=5,
Down=5

52: What does the Padding Property represent?
Answer:
It represents the distance between the control's border and its content(s).

53: What kind of controls have Margin Property (What do they have to derive from)?

Answer:

All the controls that derive from FrameworkElement have a Margin Property

54: What kind of controls have PaddingProperty (What do they have to derive from)?

Answer:

All the controls that derive from Control, Border or TextBox have a Margin Property

55: How do you create a password field in Silverlight?

Answer:

By using the PasswordBox, which behaves just like a TextBox except that the input is not visible.

56: How can you change the character that is displayed in a Password Field?

Answer:

By specifying its PasswordChar property and giving it a new character.

PasswordChar="*"

57: You have the following code:

```
<Checkbox IsChecked="{Binding Chk}" />
<TextBox Text="Check me" />
```

This shows a checkbox and text next to it

What would be the easier way to do this (which requires fewer controls to be used)?

Answer:

Specifying the Content property of the Checkbox.

```
<Checkbox IsChecked="{Binding Chk}" Content="Check me" />
```

58: What controls does a UserControl contain when creating a new one (besides the namespace declarations)?

Answer:
It contains a Grid to hold further controls

59: What is the default name of the Grid that is created when a new UserControl is added to the project?
Answer:
The Grid has an x:Name property of "LayoutRoot"

60: How can you make a Grid's background transparent?
Answer:
By setting it is Background property to Transparent instead of specifying an actual color
Background="Transparent"

61: Give an example that uses a hyperlink in Silverlight.
Answer:
<HyperlinkButton Content="Contact"
Click="Click_eventHandler" />

62: How can you hide a control in Silverlight?
Answer:
By specifying it is Visibility property to Collapsed

63: What are the possible values of the Visibility property?
Answer:
The possible values are Visible and Collapsed

64: What would you need to do if you have a Boolean property and you would need to show or hide a control based on that Boolean?
<Button Visibility="{Binding myBoolean}" />
Answer:
You would need to create a value converter that takes a Boolean and returns the appropriate Visibility, then use the converter inside the binding
<Button Visibility="{Binding myBoolean,

Converter={StaticResource BoolToVisibilityConverter}}" />

65: If you have a ComboBox, how can you see which element is selected?
Answer:
By using the SelectedItem, SelectedValue or SelectedIndex properties

66: If you have a ComboBox, how can you see when the selected item is changed?
Answer:
By using the SelectionChanged event
<ComboBox SelectionChanged="ComboBox_SelectionChanged" />

67: What is the difference between SelectedItem and SelectedIndex when using a ComboBox?
Answer:
SelectedItem contains an item that is selected as an object type, SelectedIndex returns an integer value, which specifies the position in the item source of combobox that is currently selected

68: How can you change the mouse cursor show when the mouse is over an element?
Answer:
By specifying the Cursor Property on that element
Cursor="Hand", Cursor="Eraser"

69: How can you see if a ComboBox is opened?
Answer:
By using the IsDropDownOpen property which returns TRUE if the ComboBox is opened

70: How can you disable a button, so the user cannot click it anymore?
Answer:

By setting the IsEnabled property to FALSE

71: If you have a ListBox, how can you allow the user to select more than one item at a time?
Answer:
By setting the SelectionMode property to "Multiple"

72: What are the possible values of SelectionMode in a ListBox?
Answer:
The possible values are: Extended, Multiple and Single

73: What is the UpdateSourceTrigger property used for?
Answer:
In the case of a TwoWay binding, this property specifies when the data from the UI should be transmitted to the source.

74: What are the possible values of the UpdateSourceTrigger property in Silverlight and what do they mean?
Answer:
Explicit: no action is taken in updating the binding source until it is specified in the code
Default: the source of the binding is updated as soon as the control looses focus (ex: for a TextBox). This is equal to the LostFocus mode from WPF
WPF also has the option to update the source as soon as the Property is changed (PropertyChanged mode)

75: Give an example of a binding that uses ElementName and Path at the same time.
Answer:
<ComboBox x:name="combo" ItemSource="{Binding MySource}"/>
<TextBlock Text="{Binding ElementName=combo, Path=SelectedItem}" />
This uses TextBlock to show the currently selected item.

76: How can you set a TextBox that is resizable to not exceed 100 pixels in height and 200 in width?
Answer:
By setting the MaxWidth and MaxHeight properties
<TextBox MaxHeight="100" MaxWidth="200" />

77: How can you set the font of a TextBox to Arial?
Answer:
<TextBox FontFamily="Arial" />

78: What are the possible values of the TextWrapping property of a TextBox?
Answer:
NoWrap and Wrap (doesn't allow the text inside the TextBox to exceed the textbox's width)

79: How do you color a Border in Red?
Answer:
<Border BorderBrush="Red" />

80: What are the ways to make RadioButtons belong to the same group (so that their selection is mutually exclusive)?
Answer:
   a)   Assign the same GroupName in the properties
   b)   Place them inside the same container

81: When using a DataGrid, how can you allow the user to sort the DataGrid's columns?
Answer:
By setting the CanUserSortColumns="True"

82: While using a DataGrid, how can you allow the user to reorder the DataGrid's columns?
Answer:
By setting the CanUserReorderColumns="True"

83: When using a DataGrid, how can you allow the user to resize the DataGrid's columns?
Answer:
By setting the CanUserResizeColumns="True"

84: When using a DataGrid, how can you auto prevent the auto generation of Columns?
Answer:
By setting the AutoGenerateColumns="False"

85: When using a DataGrid, what are the possible values of the ClipboardCopyMode property?
Answer:
The possible values are:
   a) ExcludeHeader
   b) IncludeHeader
   c) None

86: In a DataGrid, how can you only show the row details when the user has selected a row?
Answer:
By using the RowDetailsVisibilityMode property to VisibleWhenSelected

87: What are the possible values of RowDetailsVisibilityMode in a DataGrid?
Answer:
The possible values are:
   a) VisibleWhenSelected
   b) Visible
   c) Collapsed

88: How can you show only the Vertical gridlines in a DataGrid?
Answer:
By setting the GridLinesVisibility property to "Vertical"

89: What are the possible values for GridLinesVisibility in a DataGrid?

Answer:

The possible values are:

a) All

b) None

c) Horizontal

d) Vertical

90: In what assembly is the DataGrid found?

Answer:

System.Windows.Controls.Data

91: What are the three types of DataGrid Columns?

Answer:

The three types of DataGrid Columns are:

a) DataGridTemplateColumn

b) DataGridTextColumn

c) DataGridCheckBoxColumn

92: What is the property that you use to set the column name (the one visible to the user) on a DataGrid Column?

Answer:

The Header property

Header="Name"

93: How can you allow or deny a user to resize a specific column in a DataGrid?

Answer:

By setting the CanUserResize to TRUE or FALSE on the specified column.

Enhancing the User Interface

94: What kind of property is the Style property?
Answer:
It is a dependency property, because it can be databound, and it can have property changed notifications (as opposed to a CLR property)

95: How do you access a resource from code-behind?
Answer:
This is achieved by using Resources[key] and casting it to the appropriate one

96: Give an example of a simple style for a Button.
Answer:
```
<style x:Key="myStyle" TargetType="Button">
<setter Property="Foreground" Value="Blue">
</style>
<Button Style="{StaticResource myStyle}"/>
```

97: What kind of properties can have a Style applied to them?
Answer:
Dependency properties can have a Style applied to them.

98: In what region of the XAML do the Styles need to be declared?
Answer:
In the Resources region (Usercontrol, Grid, Central Application resources, etc.)

99: How can you make a style to be automatically applied to all controls of one type?
Answer:
By not specifying a x:Key property. This makes the style apply to every TargetType control it can.

100: If you have a Style with no x:Key property defined at the UserControl level, and another one defined in a grid that is

contained in the UserControl, which Style will "win"?
Answer:
The style declared "closer" to the control, in this case the style declared on the Grid

101: Where do you have to declare a Style in order for it to be available in the entire application?
Answer:
In the App.XAML - Application.Resources region

102: How would you combine multiple styles on the same control?
Answer:
By using the BasedOn="{StaticResource styleName}" on different styles, to make them build on top of each other.

103: How would you change the content of a button to contain an image and a textbox?
Answer:
<Button>
<Button.Content>
<StackPanel>
<Image/>
<TextBox/>
</StackPanel>
</Button.Content>
</Button>

104: Give an example of a Rotation transform applied to a button.
Answer:
<Button>
<Button.RenderTransform>
<RotateTransform Angle="20" />
</Button.RenderTransform>
</Button>

105: Give an example of a Scale transform applied to a button.
Answer:

```
<Button>
<Button.RenderTransform>
<ScaleTransform ScaleX="2" />
</Button.RenderTransform>
</Button>
```

106: Give four examples of possible transforms that can be applied to a button.
Answer:

a) Translation
b) Scale
c) Rotation
d) Skew

Implementing Application Logic

107: What are Routed Events?

Answer:

A Routed Event is an event that is potentially passed on (routed) from a child object to each of its successive parent objects in the object tree.

An event that is passed to each of its parent object from a child object in the object tree.

108: What kind of routing do the events in Silverlight have?

Answer:

Either NO routing or "bubbling" routing. The Silverlight events do not have the "tunneling" behavior

109: What is the Handled property of RoutedEventArgs used for?

Answer:

It indicates whether an routed event has been handled, thus causing it to not "bubble" anymore

110: How can you handle routed events on a Popup or Tooltip?

Answer:

By placing an event handler on elements that are inside the Popup or Tooltip, because routed events only work for elements on the main visual tree. The Popup and Tooltip are not considered this way and they never receive routed events

111: Why is user-initiated event needed to be called as soon as possible in an event handler?

Answer:

It is because Silverlight's mechanism has a period of approximately one second when the user-initiated event can be called. These events include OpenFileDialog, SaveFileDialog, and the PrintDialog.

112: How do you remove an event handler in Silverlight?

Answer:

By using the C# syntax to remove event handlers ("= "):
txtbox.MouseLeftButtonDown -= txtbox_MouseLeftButtonDown;
or the VB syntax:
RemoveHandler txtbox.MouseLeftButtonDown , AddressOf
txtbox_MouseLeftButtonDown

**113: When adding a new routed event by using public void
AddHandler(RoutedEvent routedEvent, Delegate handler,bool
handledEventsToo),
What does the handledEventsToo mean?**
Answer:
It means that the handler will be invoked even if some other
element marked the event as handled before it reached this point.

**114: When accessing a WCF service from Silverlight, which
file(s) needs to be created in the root directory of the WCF
service in order to enable cross domain policy?**
Answer:
clientaccesspolicy.xml and crossdomain.xml

115: What is the purpose of Dependency properties?
Answer:
Their purpose is to compute the value of a property based on the
value of other inputs (themes, data binding, etc)

**116: What is the difference between WPF browser application
and Silverlight?**
Answer:
In order for WPF browser apps to run, the client computer needs
.NET framework installed, while for the Silverlight app to run,
you only need the browser plug-in.

**117: How can you enable cancellation while a
BackgroundWorker is doing its task?**
Answer:
By calling the CancelAsync on the background worker, and by

checking the background worker's CancellationPending in the DoWork handler of the worker.

118: How can you see the progress of a task executed in a BackgroundWorker?
Answer:
By using its ProgressChanged event to update the UI.

119: What should you use in order to update the UI from a background thread?
Answer:
You should use the Dispatcher class which gets back to the UI, thus allowing the UI to change.

120: How does the update of the UI work in Silverlight from the multithreading point of view?
Answer:
The only thread that allows updates to be performed on the UI is the main thread (the UI one). In order to update the UI from a background thread you must use the Dispatcher class which allows changes to be made to the UI.

121: How would you declare a Dependency Property?
Answer:
```
public string my_Name1
{
    public static readonly DP my_Name_Property1property =
    DP.Register("my_Name_Property1", typeof(string),
    typeof(my_Name1),
    new PropertyMetadata(""));
}
// To set and get values
Public String my_Name_Property1{
        set {
        this.SV (my_Name_Property1property, value); }
    get { return (string) this.GV (my_Name1Propertyproperty); }
```

}

DP ⟶ DependencyProperty
SV ⟶ SetValue
GV ⟶ GetValue

122: How do you set a default value for a Dependency Property?
Answer:
By specifying the new PropertyMetadata("DefaultValue") in the Register method

123: What are attached properties?
Answer:
Attached properties allow child elements to set values to properties defined on their parents

124: Give an example of an Attached Property.
Answer:
Grid.Row, Canvas.Top are examples of an Attached Property.

125: How do you set the value of an attached property in code-behind?
Answer:
By using the SetValue method on the UI element, with the following parameters: the attached property and the value.

126: What interface do you need to implement in order to add custom Commands?
Answer:
You need to implement the ICommand interface

127: Give an example of command binding for a button.
Answer:
<Button Command="{Binding MyCommand}" />

128: What is XAML?
Answer:

XAML is a declarative language based on XML with which you can define objects and properties in XML

Working with Data

129: In Silverlight 4, what does an object have to derive from to be able to be DataBound?
Answer:
It has to derive from DependencyObject. Previously it was required that the object derived from the FrameworkElement class

130: How do you format strings in XAML? Give an example.
Answer:
<TextBlock Text="{Binding Date, StringFormat='MM dd yyyy'}"/>

131: How do you specify the value to be shown if the property that is used for binding is null?
Answer:
By specifying the TargetNullValue='value' on the binding
<TextBlock Text="{Binding Name,TargetNullValue='no name"}"/>

132: How do you specify the value to be shown if the property that is used for binding cannot be loaded through data binding (the property does not exist or the DataContext is null)?
Answer:
By specifying the FallbackValue=' value' on the binding
<TextBlock Text="{Binding Name,FallbackValue='none"}"/>

133: What interfaces do you need to use in order to show errors on the UI?
Answer:
The interfaces needed in order to show errors on the UI are:
   a)   IDataErrorInfo
   b)   INotifyDataErrorInfo

134: What interface does a collection need to implement in order for it to be able to notify changes made to its elements?
Answer:
It needs to implement the INotifyCollectionChanged

135: What collection type automatically notifies changes made to

its elements?

Answer:

ObservableCollection<T> already implements the INotifyCollectionChanged

136: What interface does a non-collection item have to implement in order for it to be able to notify changes performed on it?

Answer:

It has to implement the INotifyPropertyChanged interface. This interface requires that an object implements the PropertyChanged event.

137: How do you use a Convertor in XAML (creation + usage)?

Answer:

You first need to create the convertor. This is done by implementing the IValueConverter interface. This gives you the Convert and ConvertBack methods. Implement those methods with the logic that you need in order to convert properly. You need to add the converter as a resource, by giving it a x:Key, and then, when the binding occurs, use the convertor as follows:
<TextBox Text="{Binding Date, Converter={StaticResource dateConverter}}" />

138: How can you specify a parameter for a Converter when using one?

Answer:

By using the ConverterParameter='value' in the binding that has the converter
<TextBox Text="{Binding Date, Converter={StaticResource dateConverter}, ConverterParameter=' mm dd'}" />

139: For what Data Binding Mode is validation a concern?

Answer:

Only for TwoWay data bindings, since the others don't need to put data back into the model

140: What are the Data Binding Modes in Silverlight?
Answer:
The Data Binding Modes in Silverlight are:
    a) OneTime
    b) OneWay
    c) TwoWay

141: Explain OneTime Data binding mode.
Answer:
The UI is updated when the binding is created in OneTime data binding mode.

142: Explain OneWay Data binding mode.
Answer:
The UI is updated when the binding is created and when the source changes. This is the default data binding mode

143: Explain TwoWay Data binding mode.
Answer:
The UI is updated when the binding is created and when the source changes. This also updates the source when the UI (the target) changes

144: How can you disable automatic source updating when using the TwoWay Data binding mode?
Answer:
By setting the UpdateSourceTrigger=Explicit in the binding. This will only update the source when the UpdateSource method is called explicitly. This is suitable for completing forms which have a Submit button

Interacting with a Host Platform

145: What are the steps that need to be performed in order to print a page from Silverlight?
Answer:
The steps that need to be performed in order to print a page from Silverlight are:
a) Create a new PrintDocument
b) Give the print job a name with DocumentName (optional)
c) Implement the PrintPage event handler. Set the PageVisual to the UIElement that needs to be printed
d) Call the Print() method to pen the Print Dialog box

146: How do you create an out of browser application?
Answer:
By going into the Silverlight project Properties, and under the Silverlight tab, checking Enable running application out of browser.

147: What permission do you need in order to use COM Interop in Silverlight?
Answer:
You need Elevated trust permissions to run the application

148: What classes can you use to access Isolated storage from Silverlight?
Answer:
You can use IsolatedStorageSettings for key/value pairs or IsolatedStorageFIle for working with files

149: What kind of representation do the settings have in Isolated storage when using IsolatedStorageSettings class?
Answer:
They have a Dictionary representation aka key/value pairs.

150: Which are the methods you would typically use when working with IsolatedStorageSettings class?
Answer:

a) **Add:** add an entry in the dictionary
b) **Contains:** check if a specific key exists
c) **Remover:** remove an entry from the dictionary

151: Which is the method that you use in order to increase the Isolated storage quota?
Answer:
You must use the IsolatedStorageFile class with the method IncreaseQuotaTo(long value). This returns TRUE if the operation succeeded or FALSE if it didn't.

152: How do you access query strings?
Answer:
By using the HtmlPage.QueryString["key"]

153: How do you call a JavaScript method from Silverlight?
Answer:
By using HtmlPage.Window.Invoke() function, with the function name and the function parameter as parameters

154: How can you access a Silverlight method from JavaScript?
Answer:
By making a call to RegisterScriptableObject() in the Silverlight app constructor (this registers a managed object for scriptable access by JavaScript code.
The function you want to call in Silverlight must be prefixed with the [ScriptableMember] attribute. Then, in JavaScript use the following
var control = document.getElementById("silverlightControl");
control.Content.Page.MyFunction("Hello from JavaScript!");

155: How can you set text in the clipboard when using Silverlight?
Answer:
Using the Clipboard.SetText(string text) method

156: How can you get text from the clipboard when using Silverlight?
Answer:
Using the Clipboard.GetText() method

157: How can you save a file inSilverlight?
Answer:
By using the SaveFileDialog

158: How can you open a file in Silverlight?
Answer:
By using the OpenFileDialog

159: How can you provide Notification (toast) messages in Silverlight?
Answer:
By using the NotificationWindow, setting its content property to the control you want to show, and calling the Show method with the number of milliseconds the notification window should be shown

160: How can you make the text in a Texbox to be shown from the right to the left?
Answer:
By giving the FlowDirection property a value of RightToLeft

161: What do you need to enable in order to be able to drag and drop a file from the desktop or file explorer onto the Silverlight Application?
Answer:
The AllowDrop attribute must be set to TRUE on the targeted UIElement.

162: How can you set file filtering when using the OpenFileDialog?
Answer:

With the help of the Filter and FilterIndex properties

163: How will you load the Silverlight application in Html/Aspx?
Answer:
Using 'object' tag. It is loaded inside Html by pointing to the path to load XAP (a Silverlight application). Object tag intimate the browser to set the Silverlight plug-in. Inside the object tag, using 'params' a Java script function can be called, background colors can be specified, plug-in can be automatically updated, etc.
Example:
```
<object data= "">
    <params name "my_src1" value= "my fold/abc.xap"/>
    ...
</object>
```

164: What is Isolated Storage?
Answer:
Large Temporary Storage Mechanism which utilizes three files to manage the contents and is cleared when a user deletes the browser cache. These files are well documented so a hacker can easily access it. Thus the contents of isolated storage are insecure.

165: How will you set the minimum required version and automatic update of a Silverlight application?
Answer:
In HTML, XAP is load using object tag. In that, using params required version and automatic update can be set.
Example:
```
<Object>
    <Params name= "minRuntimeVersion" value= "Req
    version number"/>
    <Params name= "autoUpgrade" value= "True">
</Object>
```

166: What are the ways to add content inside the 'main Page'?

Answer:

The ways to add content in the 'Main Page' are:

a) Declarative approach XAML

Silverlight controls are used in xml format and uses properties as attributes

b) Programmatic approach in code behind

Objects are created programmatically and the properties are set

167: How will you display a text using the declarative approach?

Answer:

In the 'main Page', add the following lines of code in the grid tag.

Example:

```
<Grid x:Name= "my_app" Background= "Blue">
<TextBlock x: Name= "My_txt1" Text= "Hello user" ForeGround =
"White" HorizontalAlignment= "Center"/>
</Grid>
```

168: How will you display a text using 'programmatic approach'?

Answer:

To display the text, textblock instance should be created in the constructor of the "main Page".

Example:

```
TextBlock my_txtblk = new TextBlock
{
Name = "my_txtblk",
Text = "Hello User",
ForeGround = new SolidBrush(colors.White),
HorizontalAlignment = HorizontalAlignment.Center
};
```

169: What is the function of 'User control' tag?

Answer:

User Control tag is created using XAML and has only one child as a control. It is the root of the user's XAML and reused in various

places.
Example:
<User Control x: class = "SilverlightApps. My_first_App. Main
Page"…. >
</User Control>

170: What is the way to create a table format in the Usercontrol?
Answer:
Using Grid panel.
Example:
```
<Grid x:= "my_Layout1" BackGround= "Blue">
    <Grid.RowDefinitions>
        < RowDefinitions/>
        <Grid.RowDefinitions/>
    <Grid.ColumnDefinitions>
        < ColumnDefinitions/>
        <ColumnDefinitions/>
    <Grid. ColumnDefinitions/>
    <TextBlock x:Name= "Label_My_name" Text= "My_name"
    Grid.row= "0" Grid.column= "0"/>
    <TextBlock x:Name= "My_name" Text= "Ice" Grid.row= "0"
    Grid.column= "1"/>
    <TextBlock x:Name= "Label_Status" Text= "Status" Grid.row=
    "1" Grid.column= "0"/>
    <TextBlock x:Name= "Status" Text= "Kool" Grid.row= "1"
    Grid.column= "1"/>
</Grid>
```

This page is intentionally left blank

Structuring Applications

171: How do you make sample data accessible to controls in the designer?
Answer:
By applying the DesignData build action to the sample data file and reference the file in the DesignData attribute.

172: How do you set the design time Data Context to a control?
Answer:
By using d:DataContext instead of just DataContext

173: What is a Resource Dictionary and what is it used for?
Answer:
A Resource Dictionary is, as it name states, a Dictionary that contains resources that can be used by controls in a Silverlight Application.

174: How do you declare Resources for a framework element?
Answer:
<frameworkElement>
<frameworkElement.Resources>
resources
</frameworkElement.Resources>
</frameworkElement>

175: What can you say about resource declaration from their x:Key point of view?
Answer:
Every resource must have a unique x:Key value in order for it to be accessed in the application.

176: How do you declare a Merged Resource Dictionary?
Answer:
<ResourceDictionary>
    <ResourceDictionary.MergedDictionaries>
        <ResourceDictionary Source="uri" />

...

</ResourceDictionary.MergedDictionaries>

</ResourceDictionary>

177: When declaring a Merged Resource dictionary, which attribute do you use to reference the other dictionary?
Answer:
You use the Source attribute, by specifying its URI.

178: What is generic.XAML?
Answer:
It is a special implementation used for controls that incorporate a Resource Dictionary.

179: What is the StaticResource markup extension used for?
Answer:
It is used to reference an already defined resource by its x:Key:
Text="{Binding text, Convertor={StaticResource MyConvertor}}"

180: How can you detect when an application shuts down?
Answer:
By handling the Exit event at the Application level
<Application Exit="handler"/>

181: What event occurs when the application starts?
Answer:
The Application Startup event
<Application Startup="handler"/>

182: How can you handle exceptions that were unhandled in the application?
Answer:
By using the UnhandledException event handler
<Application UnhandledException ="handler"/>

183: What do you have to do in order to prevent an exception

from getting to the onError handler in JavaScript?
Answer:

Set the Handled property of that exception to TRUE. If it is FALSE, it will bubble up.

Deploying Applications

184: What is the property that you use to check for Initialization parameters in a Silverlight App?
Answer:
In the Application Startup event handler, you can check for e.InitParams

185: How are the InitParams represented?
Answer:
They are represented as Dictionaries.

186: Can you check for InitParams in any other place in the application except the Startup event?
Answer:
No, because only the StartupEventArgs contain the InitParams property.

187: What is the property you use to see if the Silverlight plug-in is displayed as a windowless plug-in (in JavaScript)?
Answer:
The Windowless property.
value=silverlightObject.settings.Windowless

188: What is the property you use to get or set the background color of the Silverlight object (in JavaScript)?
Answer:
The Background property
value = silverlightObject.settings.Background;
silverlightObject.settings.Background = colorValue;

189: How do you enable GPU acceleration for Silverlight (from JavaScript)?
Answer:
By setting the silverlightObject.settings.enableGPUAcceleration.

190: What is the default value of GPU acceleration?
Answer:

The default value is FALSE

191: How do you set the Maximum frame rate of a Silverlight Application (from JavaScript)?
Answer:
By using the MaxFrameRate property
silverlightObject.settings.MaxFrameRate

192: What is the default maximum frame rate for a Silverlight Application?
Answer:
The default frame rate is 60

193: How can you see the frame rate of the current Silverlight Application?
Answer:
By setting the EnableGPUAcceleration and EnableFramerateCounter to TRUE

This page is intentionally left blank

Panels

194: What are the layout management panels?

Answer:

The layout management panels are:

a) **Canvas:** Contents can be layered and placed anywhere in the canvas

b) **Stack:** Contents are placed vertically or horizontally

c) **Grid:** Present in every xaml once the user controls are created

d) **Border:** Contains only one child

195: How will display a rectangle partially blocking the other rectangle?

Answer:

Using Z-index property. The rectangle that has the Z-index value='2', blocks the other rectangle.

Example:

```
<Canvas Background= "Blue">
    <Rectangle x:Name= "my_rect1" Fill= "White" Height= "90"
    Width= "130" canvas.left= "60"
        Canvas.Top= "60" Canvas.ZIndex= "1" />
    <Rectangle x:Name= "my_rect2" Fill= "Yellow" Height= "110"
    Width= "160" canvas.left= "90"
        Canvas.Top= "70" Canvas.ZIndex= "2" />
</Canvas>
```

196: How will you display the text inside the 'Border'?

Answer:

a) Using 'Border' layer panel, create a border of required specification

b) Inside the Border tag, create the textblock

Example:

```
<Border CornerRadius= "30" Background= "Blue">
    <TextBlock Text= "Hellllo" HorizontalAlignment=
    "Center"/>
</Border>
```

197: What happens when a stretch is set to 'Fill' or 'None' in viewbox panel?

Answer:

Fill:

a) Content will be displayed in the entire space of the view box

b) No preservation of aspect ratio is made
   Example: <Viewbox Strech=Fill>...

None:

a) Contents will be displayed in its original size
   Example: <Viewbox Strech=None>...

198: What happens when a stretch is set to 'Uniform' or 'UniformToFill' in viewbox panel?

Answer:

Uniform:

a) Content will be displayed by resizing depending on the viewbox size

b) Takes the space required to display the content
   Example: <Viewbox Strech= Uniform >...

UniformToFill:

a) If the content size differs from the aspect ration, the contents are clipped to viewbox size
   Example: <Viewbox Strech= UniformToFill >...

This page is intentionally left blank

Controls

199: How will you display different text with different font attributes in the textblock?

Answer:

Using 'LineBreak' and 'Run' element.

Example:

```
<TextBlock>
    <LineBreak/>
        <Run FontSize= "25" FontFamily= "Verdana">
        Helllllo</Run>
    <LineBreak/>
        <Run FontSize= "10" FontFamily= "Calibri"> Good
        Morning1</Run>
</TextBlock>
```

200: How will you create 'TextBox' in Silverlight?

Answer:

a) Using 'TextBox' tag. It is the child of 'Windows.Controls'

b) Used to get input from the user

Example:

```
<TextBox Height="133" Width= "212" Text =
"Helllllllo…Your Text"/>
```

201: What is the purpose of 'AcceptReturns' property in the Textbox?

Answer:

The hard line break is explicitly inserted when the AcceptReturns property is set to 'True'

Example:

```
<TextBox AcceptReturns="True"/>
```

202: What is the purpose of 'IsReadOnlyProperty' property in the Textbox?

Answer:

It makes the text readable only to the user.

Example:

```
<TextBox my_Property ="True"/>
```

my_Property ⟶ IsReadOnlyProperty

203: How will you set the background color and maximum length of the text?

Answer:

Using 'SolidColorBrush' and 'MaximumLength' Property.

SolidColorBrush

(TextBox.my_prprty, new SolidColorBrush(Colors.Green));

my_prprty ⟶ SelectionBackgroundProperty ,

MaxLengthProperty

MaximumLength

(TextBox.my_prprty, 133)

my_prprty ⟶ MaxLengthProperty

204: How will you create a password field in silverlight application?

Answer:

a) Using 'PasswordBox'. It is present inside the 'windows.Control'

b) Example:

<PasswordBox Width= "222" Height = "11" Password= "ice_ks" >

205: Which is the default password character and how will you change the default character?

Answer:

a) Default Character is '*'

b) To change the default character, set the required character in the passwordbox

<PasswordBox Width= "222" Height = "11" Password= "ice_ks" **PasswordChar**= "@">

206: What is the purpose of 'RichTextBox'?

Answer:

a) It is similar to the 'TextBox'

b) User can use the required format for the text

c) Example:
<RichTextBox>
    <Paragaph>
        <Bold>My_Txt_Bold</Bold>
        </LineBreak>
        <Undeline> My_Txt_Underlned</Undeline>
    </Paragaph>
    <ParagaphTextAlignment= "Center">
        CenterAlined_Content
    </Paragaph>
<RichTextBox>

207: Describe about Combo box.
Answer:
Combo box:
a) Shows the box containing list of items
b) Allows to select only one item at a time
c) Example:
<ComboBox Width= "111" >
    <ComboBox.Items>
        <ComboboxItem content= "my_list1"/>
        <ComboboxItem content= "my_list2"/>
        ...
    <ComboBox.Items>
<ComboBox/>

208: Describe about 'MaxDropDownHeight' and 'DropDownOpen'property of ComboBox.
Answer:
a) MaxDropDownHeight:
    Sets the maximum height of the dropdown
    Example:
    <ComboBox Width= "111" MaxDropDrownList= "7">
b) IsDropDownOpen:
    Set to false by default, displays the list when the arrow is clicked. Automatically displays the list when set to

'True'

209: What happen when a Editable property is set to 'True' in combo box?
Answer:
   a) The Editable is set to 'false' by default in combobox. Hence the user cannot add text in the combo box
   b) When set to true, allows the user to add text
   c) Example:
      <ComboBox Width= "111" IsEditable = "True" >

210: Describe about the ListBox.
Answer:
ListBox:
   a) Displays the list of items to the user for selection
   b) It is under 'Windows.control' namespace
   c) The properties of the listBox are 'SelectionMode' , 'ItemContainerStyle' and 'SelectionActive'

211: What are the modes of 'SelectionMode' property of listbox?
Answer:
The modes of 'SelectionMode' property of listbox are:
   a) **Single:** Allows the user to select a single item from the list
   b) **Multiple:** Allows the user to multiple items from the list
   c) **Extended:** Allows the user to select multiple items from the list using Modifier key

212: Describe about the checkbox and its states.
Answer:
   a) Allows the user to select the multiple items
   b) The states are:
      i) **Checked Item**: Returns true for the checked items
      ii) **Unchecked:** Returns false for the checked items
      iii) **Null:** Return null

213: What is the purpose of 'DataPager'?

Answer:
   a) Displays the specified number of records in a page
   b) It is used with Datgrid
   c) Example:
         <sdk DataPager x:Name= "my_datapgr1" PageSize =
         "3" />

214: Give an example to create a slider.
Answer:
<Slider x:Name= "my_slider2" ValueChanged=
"Slider_ValueChanged" Maximum= "99" Minimum = "33"/>
<TextBlock x: Name = "My_txt1" Text = "elected val"/>
Function Definition for 'slidercontrol'
private void Slider_ValueChanged(Object my_sender1,
RoutedPropertyChangedEventArgs ae){
      this.My_txt1.Text = "Selected val" + ae.NewValue.toString();
}

215: Describe about Radio Button.
Answer:
   a) Allows the user to select a single item from the displayed
      list
   b) To provide multiple selection, items should be grouped.
      So user can select one item from each group
      Example:
            <RadioButtonIsChecked = "False" Content=
            "my_contents1"/>
            ...
            <RadioButtonGroupName= "My_Grp1" Content =
            "my_content3"/>

**216: Give an example to set the instance of TextBlock and also
its properties.**
Answer:
TextBlock topHeading = new TextBlock
{

Name = "topHeading", Text = "Good Luck", FontSize = 16,
Foreground = new SolidColorBrush (Colors. Blue),
VerticalAlignment = VerticalAlignment. Left
};

217: Explain uc tag with an example.
Answer:
uc is a pre tag and is used to specify Namespace. Any name can be
used to specify it.
Example:

```
<Grid x: Name="Origin" Background="Yellow">
<uc: List View Width="170" Height="30" >
</Grid>
```

Here, uc ⟶ usercontrol

218: Give an example to create two rectangles with coordinate position (100, 200), (300,400) inside the canvas.
Answer:

```
<Canvas Background="Blue">
< Rectangle x: Name="my_1First" Fill="Black" Height="66"
Width="112"Canvas.Left="99" Canvas.Top="200"/>
   <Rectangle x:Name="my_2Second" Fill="White"
   Height="88"
   Width="277"Canvas.Left="222"Canvas.Top="399"/>
</Canvas>
```

219: Create a Button and set the background to Red.
Answer:

```
<Button Content= "Click_me1" width="199" Height= "57" style="
{StaticResource btnStyle}"/>
<Setter Property= "Background" Value= "Red"/>
```

220: What is the purpose of 'TreeView'?
Answer:
Display the hierarchial items
Example:

```
<sdk: TreeView x:Name= "My_view11">
    <sdk: TreeViewItem Header= "Alphabets">
        <sdk: TreeViewItem Header= "A">
        ...
    </sdk:TreeViewItem>
    <sdk: TreeViewItem Header= "Numbers">
        <sdk: TreeViewItem Header= "1">
        ...
    </sdk:TreeViewItem>
</sdk:TreeViewItem>
```

221: How will you embed a text and rectangle inside the button?
Answer:
Using 'Rectangle' and 'TextBlock' inside the stackPanel, we can embed a text and a rectangle inside the button.
Example:

```
<Button>
<Button.Content>
<StackPanel Orientation = "Horizontal/Vertical">
    <Rectangle Fill= "Blue">
    <TextBlock Text = "My_contents2">
</StackPanel>
</ Button.Content>
<Button>
```

222: Give an example to create a checkbox inside the Button.
Answer:

```
<Button Height = "22" Width = "111" Margin = "3">
    <Button.Content>
    <CheckBox Content = "My_chkbx_Content3"/>
    </ Button.Content>
<Button>
```

223: What is the purpose of ItemsControl?
Answer:
    a) Displays the list of items retrieved from a particular

collection
b) Does not allow the users to select the items like ListBox
c) This can also be used with ItemTemplate
   Example:
   <ItemsControl ItemSource= "{my_bindings}"
   DisplayMemberPath= "my_First_Job1" />

Display the list containing only the my_First_Job1 field from the source 'my_bindings'

224: How will you display a text with each letter spaced with particular spacing?
Answer:
Using 'Character Spacing', we can disapley a text with each letter spaced with particular spacing.
Example:
   <TextBlock Text = "my_chartr_spcng_txt" CharacterSpacing = "444">

225: How will you bind two elements?
Answer:
Two elements can be bound:
a) By setting the 'Binding' property
b) When two elements are bound, changes in one element reflect in another element
c) Example:
   <Canvas>
      <TextBlock Text = "my_binding_text1"/>
      <TextBox x:Name= "my_lstnme1"/>
      <TextBlock Text = "my_binding_text2"/>
      <TextBox x:Name= "my_lstnme2" IsEnabled= "False"
      Text= "{Binding ElementName= my_lstnme1, path=
      Text}"/>
   </Canvas>

226: How will you call a function on the server side when a

button is clicked?

Answer:

Using 'click' property of the button, we can call a function on the server side when a button is clicked.

Example:

```
<Button x:Name= "my_button1" Content = "Click+me1" />
<TextBlock x:Name = "My_Txt_blk1" />
```

Method definition on the server side for the button:

```
Public void my_button1_click(Object my_sender1,
RouterEventArgs ae,)
{
My_Txt_blk1.Text = "Done!!!!!!!";
}
```

227: How will you freeze the columns of the datagrid?

Answer:

Using 'FreezeColumnCount' property, we can freeze the columns of the datagrid.

Example:

```
<sdk: DataGrid x:Name= "My_datagrid1"
AutoGenerateColumns= "True" FrozenColumnCount=
"3" />
```

'3' columns of the datagrid will be frozen.

228: What is the purpose of TargetProperty in storyboard?

Answer:

Sets the values for the property of an object.

Example:

```
<Storyboard>
    <DoubleAnimation Storyboard.TargetName="My_Rect1"
    Storyboard.TargetProperty= "Width" From=" 147" To="277"
    Duration="0:0:3" />
<Storyboard>
```

229: What are the ways to display text in silverlight?

Answer:

a) Silverlight supports both static and dynamic text
b) Static uses glyph element and dynamic uses text block

230: Describe about storyboard.
Answer:
A storyboard is:
a) A class that supports and controls animation with a timeline
b) Provides the information about an object and property for its child animations

This page is intentionally left blank

General Questions

231: What is the use of the ClientBin folder?
Answer:
This folder contains the .xap file of the Silverlight Application which will then be used in the ASP.NET application.

232: How do you change the startup page of a Silverlight application?
Answer:
Open the App.XAML.cs file
In the Application_Startup event handler, set the RootVisual property to the page that you want to be displayed.
private void Application_Startup(object sender, StartupEventArgs e)
{
this.RootVisual = new MainPage();
}

233: What is App.XAML?
Answer:
It is a file used in Silverlight applications which defines global styles, properties that can be used for passing data between XAML pages and defines event handlers for application start, exit etc

234: What are the similarities between WPF and Silverlight?
Answer:
Both Windows Presentation Foundation (WPF) and Silverlight are technologies used to create Rich user interface applications. Both these use XAML to describe the UI.

235: What is the Silverlight RunTime?
Answer:
It is a component responsible for downloading the .xap file from the server and run the code inside the xap.

236: What does RIA come from?

Answer:
Rich Internet Applications.

237: What is name of Linux version of Silverlight?
Answer:
MoonLight

238: What is the difference between WPF and Silverlight?
Answer:
Silverlight is a browser plug-in while WPF runs under Windows

239: How many XAML files are created when starting a new Silverlight project in Visual Studio?
Answer:
Two XAML files are created:
   a)   App.XAML
   b)   MainPage.XAML

240: Which programming language(s) can you use to write the code-behind for a Silverlight application?
Answer:
You can use either C# or Visual Basic.

241: Enumerate some Layout Management Panels and when you will use them?
Answer:
   a)   **Canvas Panel:** simple layouts, controls can overlap each other
   b)   **Stack Panel:** grouping controls in stacks, horizontally or vertically
   c)   **Grid Panel:** a "table" with multiple rows and columns

242: Are ADO.NET objects supported in a Silverlight Application (DataTable, DataSet, DataColumn)?
Answer:
No, they are not supported.

243: Name the methods of a MediaElement object in Silverlight.

Answer:

Play, Pause, and Stop are the methods of a MediaElement object in Silverlight.

244: Enumerate the types of Brushes in Silverlight.

Answer:

The types of brushes in Silverlight are:
   a) SolidColorBrush
   b) LinearGradientBrush
   c) RadialGradientBrush
   d) ImageBrush
   e) VideoBrush

245: Which video formats are supported in Silverlight?

Answer:

The Windows Media Audio and Video (WMA, WMV7-9) and MP3 formats are supported in Silverlight.

246: What is the XAP mime type?

Answer:

application/x-silverlight

247: What is Silverlight Toolkit?

Answer:

The Silverlight Tool kit is a collection of Silverlight Tools and Components used to develop Silverlight Applications.

248: Is Silverlight free?

Answer:

Yes, the browser plug-in is free.

249: What is the Silverlight SDK?

Answer:

The Silverlight SDK is a set of tools, documentation, samples, and templates to allow developers to easily build Silverlight

Applications.

250: What is MainPage.XAML?

Answer:

It is a default XAML file created when a new Silverlight application is created. It does not contain any UI elements

251: What is MVVM?

Answer:

Model View View-Model is a design pattern used in Silverlight application development which separates the view from the model.

This page is intentionally left blank

HR Questions

Review these typical interview questions and think about how you would answer them. Read the answers listed; you will find best possible answers along with strategies and suggestions.

1: Tell me about your favorite book or newspaper.

Answer:

The interviewer will look at your answer to this question in order to determine your ability to analyze and review critically. Additionally, try to choose something that is on a topic related to your field or that embodies a theme important to your work, and be able to explain how it relates. Stay away from controversial subject matter, such as politics or religion.

2: If you could be rich or famous, which would you choose?

Answer:

This question speaks to your ability to think creatively, but your answer may also give great insight to your character. If you answer rich, your interviewer may interpret that you are self-confident and do not seek approval from others, and that you like to be rewarded for your work. If you choose famous, your interviewer may gather that you like to be well-known and to deal with people, and to have the platform to deliver your message to others. Either way, it is important to back up your answer with sound reasoning.

3: If you could trade places with anyone for a week, who would it be and why?

Answer:

This question is largely designed to test your ability to think on your feet, and to come up with a reasonable answer to an outside the box question. Whoever you choose, explain your answer in a logical manner, and offer specific professional reasons that led you to choose the individual.

4: What would you say if I told you that just from glancing over your resume, I can already see three spelling mistakes?

Answer:

Clearly, your resume should be absolutely spotless – and you should be confident that it is. If your interviewer tries to make you second-guess yourself here, remain calm and poised and assert with a polite smile that you would be quite surprised as you are positive that your resume is error-free.

5: Tell me about your worldview.
Answer:
This question is designed to offer insight into your personality, so be aware of how the interviewer will interpret your answer. Speak openly and directly, and try to incorporate your own job skills into your outlook on life. For example, discuss your beliefs on the ways that hard work and dedication can always bring success, or in how learning new things is one of life's greatest gifts. It is okay to expand into general life principles here, but try to keep your thoughts related to the professional field as well.

6: What is the biggest mistake someone could make in an interview?
Answer:
The biggest mistake that could be made in an interview is to be caught off guard! Make sure that you don't commit whatever you answer here, and additionally be prepared for all questions. Other common mistakes include asking too early in the hiring process about job benefits, not having questions prepared when the interviewer asks if you have questions, arriving late, dressing casually or sloppily, or showing ignorance of the position.

7: If you won the $50m lottery, what would you do with the money?
Answer:
While a question such as this may seem out of place in a job interview, it is important to display your creative thinking and your ability to think on the spot. It is also helpful if you choose something admirable,

8: Is there ever a time when honesty isn't appropriate in the workplace?
Answer:

This may be a difficult question, but the only time that honesty is not appropriate in the workplace is perhaps when you're feeling anger or another emotion that is best kept to yourself. If this is the case, explain simply that it is best to put some thoughts aside, and clarify that the process of keeping some thoughts quiet is often enough to smooth over any unsettled emotions, thus eliminating the problem.

9: If you could travel anywhere in the world, where would it be?
Answer:
This question is meant to allow you to be creative – so go ahead and stretch your thoughts to come up with a unique answer. However, be sure to keep your answer professionally-minded. For example, choose somewhere rich with culture or that would expose you to a new experience, rather than going on an expensive cruise through the Bahamas.

10: What would I find in your refrigerator right now?
Answer:
An interviewer may ask a creative question such as this in order to discern your ability to answer unexpected questions calmly, or, to try to gain some insight into your personality. For example, candidates with a refrigerator full of junk food or take-out may be more likely to be under stress or have health issues, while a candidate with a balanced refrigerator full of nutritious staples may be more likely to lead a balanced mental life, as well.

11: If you could play any sport professionally, what would it be and what aspect draws you to it?
Answer:
Even if you do not know much about professional sports, this question might be a great opportunity to highlight some of your greatest professional working skills. For example, you may choose to play professional basketball, because you admire the teamwork and coordination that goes into creating a solid play. Or, you may choose to play professional tennis, because you consider yourself

to be a go-getter with a solid work ethic and great dedication to perfecting your craft. Explain your choice simply to the interviewer without elaborating on drawn-out sports metaphors, and be sure to point out specific areas or skills in which you excel.

12: Who were the presidential and vice-presidential candidates in the 2008 elections?

Answer:

This question, plain and simple, is intended as a gauge of your intelligence and awareness. If you miss this question, you may well fail the interview. Offer your response with a polite smile, because you understand that there are some individuals who probably miss this question.

13: Explain X *task* in a few short sentences as you would to a second-grader.

Answer:

An interviewer may ask you to break down a normal job task that you would complete in a manner that a child could understand, in part to test your knowledge of the task's inner workings – but in larger part, to test your ability to explain a process in simple, basic terms. While you and your coworkers may be able to converse using highly technical language, being able to simplify a process is an important skill for any employee to have.

14: If you could compare yourself to any animal, what would it be?

Answer:

Many interviewers ask this question, and it is not to determine which character traits you think you embody – instead, the interviewer wants to see that you can think outside the box, and that you are able to reason your way through any situation. Regardless of what animal you answer, be sure that you provide a thorough reason for your choice.

15: Who is your hero?

Answer:

Your hero may be your mother or father, an old professor, someone successful in your field, or perhaps even Wonder Woman – but keep your reasoning for your choice professional, and be prepared to offer a logical train of thought. Choose someone who embodies values that are important in your chosen career field, and answer the question with a smile and sense of passion.

16: Who would play you in the movie about your life?
Answer:

As with many creative questions that challenge an interviewee to think outside the box, the answer to this question is not as important as how you answer it. Choose a professional, and relatively non-controversial actor or actress, and then be prepared to offer specific reasoning for your choice, employing important skills or traits you possess.

17: Name five people, alive or dead, that would be at your ideal dinner party.
Answer:

Smile and sound excited at the opportunity to think outside the box when asked this question, even if it seems to come from left field. Choose dynamic, inspiring individuals who you could truly learn from, and explain what each of them would have to offer to the conversation. Do not forget to include yourself, and to talk about what you would bring to the conversation as well!

18: What is customer service?
Answer:

Customer service can be many things – and the most important consideration in this question is that you have a creative answer. Demonstrate your ability to think outside the box by offering a confident answer that goes past a basic definition, and that shows you have truly considered your own individual view of what it means to take care of your customers. The thoughtful consideration you hold for customers will speak for itself.

19: Tell me about a time when you went out of your way for a customer.
Answer:
It is important that you offer an example of a time you truly went out of your way – be careful not to confuse something that felt like a big effort on your part, with something your employer would expect you to do anyway. Offer an example of the customer's problems, what you did to solve it, and the way the customer responded after you took care of the situation.

20: How do you gain confidence from customers?
Answer:
This is a very open-ended question that allows you to show your customer service skills to the interviewer. There are many possible answers, and it is best to choose something that you have had great experience with, such as "by handling situations with transparency," "offering rewards," or "focusing on great communication." Offer specific examples of successes you have had.

21: Tell me about a time when a customer was upset or agitated – how did you handle the situation?
Answer:
Similarly to handling a dispute with another employee, the most important part to answering this question is to first set up the scenario, offer a step-by-step guide to your particular conflict resolution style, and end by describing the way the conflict was resolved. Be sure that in answering questions about your own conflict resolution style, that you emphasize the importance of open communication and understanding from both parties, as well as a willingness to reach a compromise or other solution.

22: When can you make an exception for a customer?
Answer:

Exceptions for customers can generally be made when in accordance with company policy or when directed by a supervisor. Display an understanding of the types of situations in which an exception should be considered, such as when a customer has endured a particular hardship, had a complication with an order, or at a request.

23: What would you do in a situation where you were needed by both a customer and your boss?
Answer:
While both your customer and your boss have different needs of you and are very important to your success as a worker, it is always best to try to attend to your customer first – however, the key is explaining to your boss why you are needed urgently by the customer, and then to assure your boss that you will attend to his or her needs as soon as possible (unless it is absolutely an urgent matter).

24: What is the most important aspect of customer service?
Answer:
While many people would simply state that customer satisfaction is the most important aspect of customer service, it is important to be able to elaborate on other important techniques in customer service situations. Explain why customer service is such a key part of business, and be sure to expand on the aspect that you deem to be the most important in a way that is reasoned and well-thought out.

25: Is it best to create low or high expectations for a customer?
Answer:
You may answer this question either way (after, of course, determining that the company does not have a clear opinion on the matter). However, no matter which way you answer the question, you must display a thorough thought process, and very clear reasoning for the option you chose. Offer pros and cons of each, and include the ultimate point that tips the scale in favor of

your chosen answer.

26: Why did you choose your college major?
Answer:
It is important to display interest in your work, and if your major is related to your current field, it will be simple for you to relate the two. Perhaps you even knew while in college that you wanted to do a job similar to this position, and so you chose the major so as to receive the education and training you needed to succeed. If your major does not relate clearly, it is still important to express a sense of passion for your choice, and to specify the importance of pursuing something that matters to you – which is how you made the decision to come to your current career field instead.

27: Tell me about your college experience.
Answer:
It is best to keep this answer positive – do not focus on parties, pizza, or procrastinating. Instead, offer a general summary of the benefits you received in college, followed by an anecdote of a favorite professor or course that opened up your way of thinking about the field you are in. This is a great opportunity for you to show your passion for your career, make sure to answer enthusiastically and confidently.

28: What is the most unique thing about yourself that you would bring to this position?
Answer:
This question is often asked as a close to an interview, and it gives you a final chance to highlight your best qualities to the employer. Treat the question like a sort of review, and explain why your specific mix of education, experience, and passions will be the ideal combination for the employer. Remain confident but humble, and keep your answer to about two minutes.

29: How did your last job stand up to your previous expectations of it?

Answer:
While it is okay to discuss what you learned if you expected too much out of a previous job, it is best to keep this question away from negative statements or portrayals. Focus your answer around what your previous job did hold that you had expected, and how much you enjoyed those aspects of the position.

30: How did you become interested in this field?
Answer:
This is the chance for you to show your passion for your career – and the interviewer will be assured that you are a great candidate if it is obvious that you enjoy your job. You can include a brief anecdote here in order to make your interest personal, but be sure that it is *brief*. Offer specific names of mentors or professors who aided in your discovery, and make it clear that you love what you do.

31: What was the greatest thing you learned while in school?
Answer:
By offering a lesson you learned outside of the classroom, you can show the interviewer your capacity for creativity, learning, and reflection. The practical lessons you learned in the classroom are certainly invaluable in their own right and may pertain closely to the position, but showing the mastery of a concept that you had to learn on your own will highlight your growth potential.

32: Tell me about a time when you had to learn a different skill set for a new position.
Answer:
Use a specific example to describe what you had to learn and how you set about outlining goals and tasks for yourself. It is important to show that you mastered the skill largely from your dedication to learning it, and because of the systematic approach you took to developing and honing your individual education. Additionally, draw connections between the skill you learned and the new position, and show how well prepared you are for the job.

33: Tell me about a person who has been a great influence in your career.

Answer:

It is important to make this answer easy to relate to – your story should remind the interviewer of the person who was most influential in his or her own career. Explain what you learned from this person and why they inspired you, and how you hope to model them later in your career with future successes.

34: What would this person tell me about you?

Answer:

Most importantly, if this person is one of your references – they had better know who you are! There are all too many horror stories of professors or past employers being called for a reference, and not being able to recall when they knew you or why you were remarkable, which does not send a very positive message to potential employers. This person should remember you as being enthusiastic, passionate, and motivated to learn and succeed.

35: What is the most productive time of day for you?

Answer:

This is a trick question – you should be equally productive all day! While it is normal to become extra motivated for certain projects, and also true that some tasks will require additional work, be sure to emphasize to the interviewer that working diligently throughout the entirety of the day comes naturally to you.

36: What was the most responsibility you were given at your previous job?

Answer:

This question provides you with an opportunity to elaborate on responsibilities that may or may not be on your resume. For instance, your resume may not have allowed room to discuss individual projects you worked on that were really outside the scope of your job responsibilities, but you can tell the interviewer here about the additional work you did and how it translated into new skills and a richer career experience for you.

37: Do you believe you were compensated fairly at your last job?
Answer:
Remember to stay positive, and to avoid making negative comments about your previous employer. If you were not compensated fairly, simply state that you believe your qualities and experience were outside the compensation limitations of the old job, and that you're looking forward to an opportunity that is more in line with the place you are at in your career.

38: Tell me about a time when you received feedback on your work, and enacted it.
Answer:
Try to give an example of feedback your received early in your career, and the steps you took to incorporate it with your work. The most important part of this question is to display the way you learned from the feedback, as well as your willingness to accept suggestions from your superiors. Be sure to offer reflection and understanding of how the feedback helped your work to improve.

39: Tell me about a time when you received feedback on your work that you did not agree with, or thought was unfair. How did you handle it?
Answer:
When explaining that you did not agree with particular feedback or felt it was unfair, you all need to justify tactfully why the feedback was inaccurate. Then, explain how you communicated directly with the person who offered the feedback, and, most importantly, how you listened to their response, analyzed it, and then came to a mutual agreement.

40: What was your favorite job, and why?
Answer:
It is best if your favorite job relates to the position you are currently applying for, as you can then easily draw connections

between why you enjoyed that job and why you are interested in the current position. Additionally, it is extremely important to explain why you have qualified the particular job as your favorite, and what aspects of it you would look for in another job, so that the interviewer can determine whether or not you are a good fit.

41: Tell me about an opportunity that your last position did not allow you to achieve.

Answer:

Stay focused on the positive, and be understanding of the limitations of your previous position. Give a specific example of a goal or career objective that you were not able to achieve, but rather than expressing disappointment over the missed opportunity, discuss the ways you're looking forward to the chance to grow in a new position.

42: Tell me about the worst boss you ever had.

Answer:

It is important to keep this answer brief, and positively focused. While you may offer a couple of short, critical assessments of your boss, focus on the things you learned from working with such an individual, and remain sympathetic to challenges the boss may have faced.

43: Tell me about a time when you worked additional hours to finish a project.

Answer:

It is important for your employer to see that you are dedicated to your work, and willing to put in extra hours when required or when a job calls for it. However, be careful when explaining why you were called to work additional hours – for instance, did you have to stay late because you set goals poorly earlier in the process? Or on a more positive note, were you working additional hours because a client requested for a deadline to be moved up on short notice? Stress your competence and willingness to give 110% every time.

44: Tell me about a time when your performance exceeded the duties and requirements of your job.

Answer:

If you are a great candidate for the position, this should be an easy question to answer – choose a time when you truly went above and beyond the call of duty, and put in additional work or voluntarily took on new responsibilities. Remain humble, and express gratitude for the learning opportunity, as well as confidence in your ability to give a repeat performance.

45: What is your driving attitude about work?

Answer:

There are many possible good answers to this question, and the interviewer primarily wants to see that you have a great passion for the job and that you will remain motivated in your career if hired. Some specific driving forces behind your success may include hard work, opportunity, growth potential, or success.

46: Do you take work home with you?

Answer:

It is important to first clarify that you are always willing to take work home when necessary, but you want to emphasize as well that it has not been an issue for you in the past. Highlight skills such as time management, goal-setting, and multi-tasking, which can all ensure that work is completed at work.

47: Describe a typical work day to me.

Answer:

There are several important components in your typical work day, and an interviewer may derive meaning from any or all of them, as well as from your ability to systematically lead him or her through the day. Start at the beginning of your day and proceed chronologically, making sure to emphasize steady productivity, time for review, goal-setting, and prioritizing, as well as some additional time to account for unexpected things that may arise.

48: Tell me about a time when you went out of your way at your previous job.

Answer:

Here it is best to use a specific example of the situation that required you to go out of your way, what your specific position would have required that you did, and how you went above that. Use concrete details, and be sure to include the results, as well as reflection on what you learned in the process.

49: Are you open to receiving feedback and criticisms on your job performance, and adjusting as necessary?

Answer:

This question has a pretty clear answer – yes – but you all need to display a knowledge as to why this is important. Receiving feedback and criticism is one thing, but the most important part of that process is to then implement it into your daily work. Keep a good attitude, and express that you always appreciate constructive feedback.

50: What inspires you?

Answer:

You may find inspiration in nature, reading success stories, or mastering a difficult task, but it is important that your inspiration is positively-based and that you are able to listen and tune into it when it appears. Keep this answer generally based in the professional world, but where applicable, it may stretch a bit into creative exercises in your personal life that, in turn, help you in achieving career objectives.

51: How do you inspire others?

Answer:

This may be a difficult question, as it is often hard to discern the effects of inspiration in others. Instead of offering a specific example of a time when you inspired someone, focus on general principles such as leading by example that you employ in your professional life. If possible, relate this to a quality that someone who inspired you possessed, and discuss the way you have modified or modeled it in your own work.

INDEX

Silverlight Interview Questions

Overview of Silverlight

1: How will you load "XAML" into the memory used by your application?

2: What are the events registered in the constructor of App.xaml.cs?

3: Where is InitialComponent () Method implemented?

4: How will you get the "App.g.i.cs" file in "my_solution?

5: List out the properties that needs to be initialized when a Silverlight control is created using createSilverlight function.

6: Which xml files are created when a new project is created in Silverlight?

7: What is the purpose of 'RootVisual Property'?

8: What events are handled by Silverlight?

9: How will you display the Silverlight application in Fullscreen mode?

10: Describe about .xap file.

11: What will happen when F5 is pressed to run the silverlight project?

Laying out a User Interface

12: What is the default value for a Grid's row height and column width?

13: If you have a Button inside a Grid that has multiple rows, how do you set the row that the current button will be placed on?

14: How do you set one row of the Grid to be twice the size of another?

15: If you have a Button inside a Grid, and did not specify any Grid.Row property on the button, what will the default value be?

16: How can you tell a control to span over multiple rows of a Grid?

17: What layout control would best fit the following behavior: Its children are ordered one after another without the need to do any other alignment?

18: What is the default orientation of a Stackpanel, Vertical or Horizontal?

19: How do you set a button to be placed exactly 10 pixels from the top of its Canvas parent?

20: Inside a canvas, how do you set one control to be on top of another?

21: How many children can a Border control have?

22: What is the property that you use if you want to set the thickness of a

Border control?

23: How do you draw the border line outside the border's bounding box?

24: How do you set the distance between a border and its child?

25: What control resizes its content by its own size?

26: What are the possible values for the VerticalAlignment property?

27: What are the possible values for the HorizontalAlignment property?

28: How do you set a Textbox's text to be Readonly in XAML?

29: What is the property that you have to set to make a Checkbox a three state checkbox?

30: Name some Content controls.

31: What is the method you use to switch pages if you are using the Navigation Framework?

32: How do you set the Title of the browser window if you are using the Navigation Framework?

33: How do you access the query string of the current page if you are using the Navigation Framework?

34: What is the property of a ListBox that specifies what Field of the listbox's ItemSource is shown to the user?

35: How can you modify the look of every item in a ListBox?

36: How do you specify a Listbox to have a Vertical and Horizontal Scrollbar?

37: How do you set the distance between the current control and its parent?

38: In a DataGrid, how do you specify that each other row has a different highlight color?

39: How do you set the visibility of a DataGrid's horizontal Scroll Bar?

40: In a DataGrid, how can you allow the user to automatically sort columns?

41: What control can you use to play a video?

42: How do you set the text color of a TextBox to Blue?

43: How do you set the text inside a TextBox to be Bold?

44: How do you set the Width of a TextBox to 150?

45: How do you set the Height of a TextBox to be based on the size of its contents?

46: How do you place a TextBlock inside a Grid on the third Row?

47: How do you place a TextBlock inside a Grid on the first Column?

48: You have a Grid with 2 rows and 5 columns. How can you make a TextBlock span on the columns 3 and 4 of the Grid?

49: What does the Margin Property represent?

50: When using the Margin property like this Margin="1,2,3,4", in what order will the margins be applied to the four directions (up, down, right, left) ?

51: When using the Margin property like this Margin="5", what will the values of the four directions (up, down, right, left) be?

52: What does the Padding Property represent?

53: What kind of controls have Margin Property (What do they have to derive from)?

54: What kind of controls have PaddingProperty (What do they have to derive from)?

55: How do you create a password field in Silverlight?

56: How can you change the character that is displayed in a Password Field?

57: You have the following code:

58: What controls does a UserControl contain when creating a new one (besides the namespace declarations)?

59: What is the default name of the Grid that is created when a new UserControl is added to the project?

60: How can you make a Grid's background transparent?

61: Give an example that uses a hyperlink in Silverlight.

62: How can you hide a control in Silverlight?

63: What are the possible values of the Visibility property?

64: What would you need to do if you have a Boolean property and you would need to show or hide a control based on that Boolean?

65: If you have a ComboBox, how can you see which element is selected?

66: If you have a ComboBox, how can you see when the selected item is changed?

67: What is the difference between SelectedItem and SelectedIndex when using a ComboBox?

68: How can you change the mouse cursor show when the mouse is over an element?

69: How can you see if a ComboBox is opened?

70: How can you disable a button, so the user cannot click it anymore?

71: If you have a ListBox, how can you allow the user to select more than one item at a time?

72: What are the possible values of SelectionMode in a ListBox?

73: What is the UpdateSourceTrigger property used for?

74: What are the possible values of the UpdateSourceTrigger property in Silverlight and what do they mean?

75: Give an example of a binding that uses ElementName and Path at the same time.

76: How can you set a TextBox that is resizable to not exceed 100 pixels in height and 200 in width?

77: How can you set the font of a TextBox to Arial?

78: What are the possible values of the TextWrapping property of a TextBox?

79: How do you color a Border in Red?

80: What are the ways to make RadioButtons belong to the same group (so that their selection is mutually exclusive)?

81: When using a DataGrid, how can you allow the user to sort the DataGrid's columns?

82: While using a DataGrid, how can you allow the user to reorder the DataGrid's columns?

83: When using a DataGrid, how can you allow the user to resize the DataGrid's columns?

84: When using a DataGrid, how can you auto prevent the auto generation of Columns?

85: When using a DataGrid, what are the possible values of the ClipboardCopyMode property?

86: In a DataGrid, how can you only show the row details when the user has selected a row?

87: What are the possible values of RowDetailsVisibilityMode in a DataGrid?

88: How can you show only the Vertical gridlines in a DataGrid?

89: What are the possible values for GridLinesVisibility in a DataGrid?

90: In what assembly is the DataGrid found?

91: What are the three types of DataGrid Columns?

92: What is the property that you use to set the column name (the one visible to the user) on a DataGrid Column?

93: How can you allow or deny a user to resize a specific column in a DataGrid?

Enhancing the User Interface

94: What kind of property is the Style property?

95: How do you access a resource from code-behind?

96: Give an example of a simple style for a Button.

97: What kind of properties can have a Style applied to them?

98: In what region of the XAML do the Styles need to be declared?

99: How can you make a style to be automatically applied to all controls of one type?

100: If you have a Style with no x:Key property defined at the

UserControl level, and another one defined in a grid that is contained in the UserControl, which Style will "win"?

101: Where do you have to declare a Style in order for it to be available in the entire application?

102: How would you combine multiple styles on the same control?

103: How would you change the content of a button to contain an image and a textbox?

104: Give an example of a Rotation transform applied to a button.

105: Give an example of a Scale transform applied to a button.

106: Give four examples of possible transforms that can be applied to a button.

Implementing Application Logic

107: What are Routed Events?

108: What kind of routing do the events in Silverlight have?

109: What is the Handled property of RoutedEventArgs used for?

110: How can you handle routed events on a Popup or Tooltip?

111: Why is user-initiated event needed to be called as soon as possible in an event handler?

112: How do you remove an event handler in Silverlight?

113: When adding a new routed event by using public void AddHandler(RoutedEvent routedEvent, Delegate handler,bool handledEventsToo),
What does the handledEventsToo mean?

114: When accessing a WCF service from Silverlight, which file(s) needs to be created in the root directory of the WCF service in order to enable cross domain policy?

115: What is the purpose of Dependency properties?

116: What is the difference between WPF browser application and Silverlight?

117: How can you enable cancellation while a BackgroundWorker is doing its task?

118: How can you see the progress of a task executed in a BackgroundWorker?

119: What should you use in order to update the UI from a background thread?

120: How does the update of the UI work in Silverlight from the multithreading point of view?

121: How would you declare a Dependency Property?

122: How do you set a default value for a Dependency Property?

123: What are attached properties?

124: Give an example of an Attached Property.

125: How do you set the value of an attached property in code-behind?

126: What interface do you need to implement in order to add custom Commands?

127: Give an example of command binding for a button.

128: What is XAML?

Working with Data

129: In Silverlight 4, what does an object have to derive from to be able to be DataBound?

130: How do you format strings in XAML? Give an example.

131: How do you specify the value to be shown if the property that is used for binding is null?

132: How do you specify the value to be shown if the property that is used for binding cannot be loaded through data binding (the property does not exist or the DataContext is null)?

133: What interfaces do you need to use in order to show errors on the UI?

134: What interface does a collection need to implement in order for it to be able to notify changes made to its elements?

135: What collection type automatically notifies changes made to its elements?

136: What interface does a non-collection item have to implement in order for it to be able to notify changes performed on it?

137: How do you use a Convertor in XAML (creation + usage)?

138: How can you specify a parameter for a Converter when using one?

139: For what Data Binding Mode is validation a concern?

140: What are the Data Binding Modes in Silverlight?

141: Explain OneTime Data binding mode.

142: Explain OneWay Data binding mode.

143: Explain TwoWay Data binding mode.

144: How can you disable automatic source updating when using the TwoWay Data binding mode?

Interacting with a Host Platform

145: What are the steps that need to be performed in order to print a page from Silverlight?

146: How do you create an out of browser application?

147: What permission do you need in order to use COM Interop in

Silverlight?

148: What classes can you use to access Isolated storage from Silverlight?

149: What kind of representation do the settings have in Isolated storage when using IsolatedStorageSettings class?

150: Which are the methods you would typically use when working with IsolatedStorageSettings class?

151: Which is the method that you use in order to increase the Isolated storage quota?

152: How do you access query strings?

153: How do you call a JavaScript method from Silverlight?

154: How can you access a Silverlight method from JavaScript?

155: How can you set text in the clipboard when using Silverlight?

156: How can you get text from the clipboard when using Silverlight?

157: How can you save a file inSilverlight?

158: How can you open a file in Silverlight?

159: How can you provide Notification (toast) messages in Silverlight?

160: How can you make the text in a Texbox to be shown from the right to the left?

161: What do you need to enable in order to be able to drag and drop a file from the desktop or file explorer onto the Silverlight Application?

162: How can you set file filtering when using the OpenFileDialog?

163: How will you load the Silverlight application in Html/Aspx?

164: What is Isolated Storage?

165: How will you set the minimum required version and automatic update of a Silverlight application?

166: What are the ways to add content inside the 'main Page'?

167: How will you display a text using the declarative approach?

168: How will you display a text using 'programmatic approach'?

169: What is the function of 'User control' tag?

170: What is the way to create a table format in the Usercontrol?

Structuring Applications

171: How do you make sample data accessible to controls in the designer?

172: How do you set the design time Data Context to a control?

173: What is a Resource Dictionary and what is it used for?

174: How do you declare Resources for a framework element?

175: What can you say about resource declaration from their x:Key poi of view?

176: How do you declare a Merged Resource Dictionary?

177: When declaring a Merged Resource dictionary, which attribute do you use to reference the other dictionary?

178: What is generic.XAML?

179: What is the StaticResource markup extension used for?

180: How can you detect when an application shuts down?

181: What event occurs when the application starts?

182: How can you handle exceptions that were unhandled in the application?

183: What do you have to do in order to prevent an exception from getting to the onError handler in JavaScript?

Deploying Applications

184: What is the property that you use to check for Initialization parameters in a Silverlight App?

185: How are the InitParams represented?

186: Can you check for InitParams in any other place in the application except the Startup event?

187: What is the property you use to see if the Silverlight plug-in is displayed as a windowless plug-in (in JavaScript)?

188: What is the property you use to get or set the background color of the Silverlight object (in JavaScript)?

189: How do you enable GPU acceleration for Silverlight (from JavaScript)?

190: What is the default value of GPU acceleration?

191: How do you set the Maximum frame rate of a Silverlight Application (from JavaScript)?

192: What is the default maximum frame rate for a Silverlight Application?

193: How can you see the frame rate of the current Silverlight Application?

Panels

194: What are the layout management panels?

195: How will display a rectangle partially blocking the other rectangle?

196: How will you display the text inside the 'Border'?

197: What happens when a stretch is set to 'Fill' or 'None' in viewbox panel?

198: What happens when a stretch is set to 'Uniform' or 'UniformToFill' in viewbox panel?

Controls

199: How will you display different text with different font attributes in the textblock?

200: How will you create 'TextBox' in Silverlight?

201: What is the purpose of 'AcceptReturns' property in the Textbox?

202: What is the purpose of 'IsReadOnlyProperty' property in the Textbox?

203: How will you set the background color and maximum length of the text?

204: How will you create a password field in silverlight application?

205: Which is the default password character and how will you change the default character?

206: What is the purpose of 'RichTextBox'?

207: Describe about Combo box.

208: Describe about 'MaxDropDownHeight' and 'DropDownOpen' property of ComboBox.

209: What happen when a Editable property is set to 'True' in combo box?

210: Describe about the ListBox.

211: What are the modes of 'SelectionMode' property of listbox?

212: Describe about the checkbox and its states.

213: What is the purpose of 'DataPager'?

214: Give an example to create a slider.

215: Describe about Radio Button.

216: Give an example to set the instance of TextBlock and also its properties.

217: Explain uc tag with an example.

218: Give an example to create two rectangles with coordinate position (100, 200), (300,400) inside the canvas.

219: Create a Button and set the background to Red.

220: What is the purpose of 'TreeView'?

221: How will you embed a text and rectangle inside the button?

222: Give an example to create a checkbox inside the Button.

223: What is the purpose of ItemsControl?

224: How will you display a text with each letter spaced with particular spacing?

225: How will you bind two elements?

226: How will you call a function on the server side when a button is clicked?

227: How will you freeze the columns of the datagrid?

228: What is the purpose of TargetProperty in storyboard?

229: What are the ways to display text in silverlight?

230: Describe about storyboard.

General Questions

231: What is the use of the ClientBin folder?

232: How do you change the startup page of a Silverlight application?

233: What is App.XAML?

234: What are the similarities between WPF and Silverlight?

235: What is the Silverlight RunTime?

236: What does RIA come from?

237: What is name of Linux version of Silverlight?

238: What is the difference between WPF and Silverlight?

239: How many XAML files are created when starting a new Silverlight project in Visual Studio?

240: Which programming language(s) can you use to write the code-behind for a Silverlight application?

241: Enumerate some Layout Management Panels and when you will use them?

242: Are ADO.NET objects supported in a Silverlight Application (DataTable, DataSet, DataColumn)?

243: Name the methods of a MediaElement object in Silverlight.

244: Enumerate the types of Brushes in Silverlight.

245: Which video formats are supported in Silverlight?

246: What is the XAP mime type?

247: What is Silverlight Toolkit?

248: Is Silverlight free?

249: What is the Silverlight SDK?

250: What is MainPage.XAML?

251: What is MVVM?

HR Questions

1: Tell me about your favorite book or newspaper.

2: If you could be rich or famous, which would you choose?

3: If you could trade places with anyone for a week, who would it be and why?

4: What would you say if I told you that just from glancing over your resume, I can already see three spelling mistakes?

5: Tell me about your worldview.

6: What is the biggest mistake someone could make in an interview?

7: If you won the $50m lottery, what would you do with the money?

8: Is there ever a time when honesty isn't appropriate in the workplace?

9: If you could travel anywhere in the world, where would it be?

10: What would I find in your refrigerator right now?

11: If you could play any sport professionally, what would it be and what aspect draws you to it?

12: Who were the presidential and vice-presidential candidates in the 2008 elections?

13: Explain X *task* in a few short sentences as you would to a second-grader.

14: If you could compare yourself to any animal, what would it be?

15: Who is your hero?

16: Who would play you in the movie about your life?

17: Name five people, alive or dead, that would be at your ideal dinner party.

18: What is customer service?

19: Tell me about a time when you went out of your way for a customer.

20: How do you gain confidence from customers?

21: Tell me about a time when a customer was upset or agitated – how did you handle the situation?

22: When can you make an exception for a customer?

23: What would you do in a situation where you were needed by both a customer and your boss?

24: What is the most important aspect of customer service?

25: Is it best to create low or high expectations for a customer?

26: Why did you choose your college major?

27: Tell me about your college experience.

28: What is the most unique thing about yourself that you would bring to this position?

29: How did your last job stand up to your previous expectations of it?

30: How did you become interested in this field?

31: What was the greatest thing you learned while in school?

32: Tell me about a time when you had to learn a different skill set for a new position.

33: Tell me about a person who has been a great influence in your career.

34: What would this person tell me about you?

35: What is the most productive time of day for you?

36: What was the most responsibility you were given at your previous job?

37: Do you believe you were compensated fairly at your last job?

38: Tell me about a time when you received feedback on your work, and enacted it.

39: Tell me about a time when you received feedback on your work that you did not agree with, or thought was unfair. How did you handle it?

40: What was your favorite job, and why?

41: Tell me about an opportunity that your last position did not allow you to achieve.

42: Tell me about the worst boss you ever had.

43: Tell me about a time when you worked additional hours to finish a project.

44: Tell me about a time when your performance exceeded the duties and requirements of your job.

45: What is your driving attitude about work?

46: Do you take work home with you?

47: Describe a typical work day to me.

48: Tell me about a time when you went out of your way at your previous job.

49: Are you open to receiving feedback and criticisms on your job performance, and adjusting as necessary?

50: What inspires you?

51: How do you inspire others?

Some of the following titles might also be handy:

1. .NET Interview Questions You'll Most Likely Be Asked
2. 200 Interview Questions You'll Most Likely Be Asked
3. Access VBA Programming Interview Questions You'll Most Likely Be Asked
4. Adobe ColdFusion Interview Questions You'll Most Likely Be Asked
5. Advanced Excel Interview Questions You'll Most Likely Be Asked
6. Advanced JAVA Interview Questions You'll Most Likely Be Asked
7. Advanced SAS Interview Questions You'll Most Likely Be Asked
8. AJAX Interview Questions You'll Most Likely Be Asked
9. Algorithms Interview Questions You'll Most Likely Be Asked
10. Android Development Interview Questions You'll Most Likely Be Asked
11. Ant & Maven Interview Questions You'll Most Likely Be Asked
12. Apache Web Server Interview Questions You'll Most Likely Be Asked
13. Artificial Intelligence Interview Questions You'll Most Likely Be Asked
14. ASP.NET Interview Questions You'll Most Likely Be Asked
15. Automated Software Testing Interview Questions You'll Most Likely Be Asked
16. Base SAS Interview Questions You'll Most Likely Be Asked
17. BEA WebLogic Server Interview Questions You'll Most Likely Be Asked
18. C & C++ Interview Questions You'll Most Likely Be Asked
19. C# Interview Questions You'll Most Likely Be Asked
20. C++ Internals Interview Questions You'll Most Likely Be Asked
21. CCNA Interview Questions You'll Most Likely Be Asked
22. Cloud Computing Interview Questions You'll Most Likely Be Asked
23. Computer Architecture Interview Questions You'll Most Likely Be Asked
24. Computer Networks Interview Questions You'll Most Likely Be Asked
25. Core JAVA Interview Questions You'll Most Likely Be Asked
26. Data Structures & Algorithms Interview Questions You'll Most Likely Be Asked
27. Data WareHousing Interview Questions You'll Most Likely Be Asked
28. EJB 3.0 Interview Questions You'll Most Likely Be Asked
29. Entity Framework Interview Questions You'll Most Likely Be Asked
30. Fedora & RHEL Interview Questions You'll Most Likely Be Asked
31. GNU Development Interview Questions You'll Most Likely Be Asked
32. Hibernate, Spring & Struts Interview Questions You'll Most Likely Be Asked
33. HTML, XHTML and CSS Interview Questions You'll Most Likely Be Asked
34. HTML5 Interview Questions You'll Most Likely Be Asked
35. IBM WebSphere Application Server Interview Questions You'll Most Likely Be Asked
36. iOS SDK Interview Questions You'll Most Likely Be Asked
37. Java / J2EE Design Patterns Interview Questions You'll Most Likely Be Asked
38. Java / J2EE Interview Questions You'll Most Likely Be Asked
39. Java Messaging Service Interview Questions You'll Most Likely Be Asked
40. JavaScript Interview Questions You'll Most Likely Be Asked
41. JavaServer Faces Interview Questions You'll Most Likely Be Asked
42. JDBC Interview Questions You'll Most Likely Be Asked
43. jQuery Interview Questions You'll Most Likely Be Asked
44. JSP-Servlet Interview Questions You'll Most Likely Be Asked
45. JUnit Interview Questions You'll Most Likely Be Asked
46. Linux Commands Interview Questions You'll Most Likely Be Asked
47. Linux Interview Questions You'll Most Likely Be Asked
48. Linux System Administrator Interview Questions You'll Most Likely Be Asked
49. Mac OS X Lion Interview Questions You'll Most Likely Be Asked
50. Mac OS X Snow Leopard Interview Questions You'll Most Likely Be Asked
51. Microsoft Access Interview Questions You'll Most Likely Be Asked

For complete list visit

www.vibrantpublishers.com

www.ingramcontent.com/pod-product-compliance
Lightning Source LLC
Chambersburg PA
CBHW060941050326
40689CB00012B/2537